Baldwinsville Public Library
33 East Genesee Street
Baldwinsville, NY 13027-2575

DEC 13 2006

WITHDRAWN

D1410718

Reading Essentials
in Science

Baldwinsville Public Library
33 East Genesee Street
Baldwinsville, NY 13027-2575

ENERGY WORKS!

Electricity
and
Magnetism

JENNY KARPELENIA

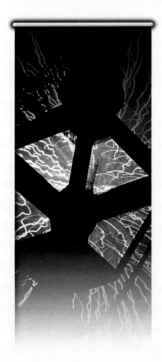

PERFECTION LEARNING®

Editorial Director:	Susan C. Thies
Editor:	Mary L. Bush
Design Director:	Randy Messer
Book Design:	Mark Hagenberg, Michelle Glass, Lori Gould
Cover Design:	Michael A. Aspengren

A special thanks to the following for their scientific review of the book:

Judy Beck, Ph.D; Associate Professor, Science Education; University of South Carolina-Spartanburg

Jeffrey Bush; Field Engineer; Vessco, Inc.

Image Credits:
©Bettmann/CORBIS: pp. 5 (right), 33 (middle), 34 (top-right); ©Robert Liewellyn/CORBIS: p. 18;
©David Arky/CORBIS: p. 20; ©Lester Lefkowitz/CORBIS: p. 29; ©Bill Varie/CORBIS: p. 35 (left);
©Roger Ressmeyer/CORBIS: p. 35 (right); ©Images.com/CORBIS: p. 32 (right)

Cover: Photos.com (front-middle, front-right, background), ArtToday (front-left), Corel (back cover);
©Royalty-Free/CORBIS: p. 10, 22; ArtToday (arttoday.com): pp. 4, 5 (left), 11 (top), 32 (left), 33 (top),
34 (top-left), all art on sidebars; Photos.com: pp. 2–3, 7 (top), 8 (top), 12, 13 (top), 15, 19, 21,
23 (bottom), 28, 30, 33 (bottom), 36; Hemera Technologies Inc: p. 17 (left); Digital Stock:
p. 11 (bottom); MapArt™: p. 23 (top), Perfection Learning Corporation: pp. 9, 16, 17 (right); Corel:
pp. 27, 34 (bottom); Dynamic Graphics/Liquid Library: p. 6; Lori Gould: pp. 8 (bottom), 13 (bottom),
14 (bottom), 15 (bottom), 24, 25, 31

DEC 1 3 2006

Text © 2004 by Perfection Learning® Corporation.
All rights reserved. No part of this book may be reproduced, stored in a retrieval
system, or transmitted in any form or by any means, electronic, mechanical,
photocopying, recording, or otherwise, without prior permission of the publisher.
Printed in the United States of America.

For information, contact
Perfection Learning® Corporation
1000 North Second Avenue, P.O. Box 500
Logan, Iowa 51546-0500.
Phone: 1-800-831-4190
Fax: 1-800-543-2745
perfectionlearning.com

2 3 4 5 6 7 PP 09 08 07 06 05 04

ISBN 0-7891-5865-5

Contents

Introduction to Energy

ENERGY—WHAT IS IT?

Was there ever a time when you felt so tired that you could not even shoot some hoops or play your favorite video game? Maybe you were feeling sick or very hungry. You probably felt as if you had no energy.

Now think of a time when you had lots of energy. You felt as if you could run, talk, ride your bike, or play games forever. Perhaps your parents or teachers even told you that you had *too much* energy.

So what is energy? What forms of energy are there?

Energy is the ability to get things done or to do work of some sort. Anything that accomplishes something is using some form of energy. When you hear the word *work*, do you think of chores around the house? *Work* actually means getting *anything* done. A football sailing through the air is using and giving off energy. A ringing doorbell is using and giving off energy. A shining lightbulb is using and giving off energy.

These examples also show some of the different forms of energy. A thrown football is an example of motion energy. A ringing doorbell is using electrical energy and giving off sound energy. A lightbulb uses electrical energy and gives off light and heat energy. Motion, electricity, sound, light, and heat are all forms of energy. These forms of energy affect our lives every day.

Carnival rides use electrical energy to create motion energy.

Albert Einstein

IT'S A LAW

Scientists perform experiments to test their **theories**, or ideas, about the world. Experiments that produce the same results over and over become scientific laws. One of these laws says that energy cannot be created or destroyed, but it can change from one form to another. This means that all around us, every day, energy is being changed from one form to another. The amount of energy in the universe stays the same, but it is constantly taking different forms.

The famous scientist Albert Einstein was a great thinker. He thought of new ideas that other people had not even imagined. He developed the equation $E = mc^2$. The E stands for "energy." The m stands for "mass" (the amount of "stuff" in an object). His idea shows that energy and mass can change back and forth. So energy can be changed into stuff, and stuff can be changed into energy.

ENERGY WORKS!

Energy is very important. It allows many types of work to be done. People have energy. Plants have energy. The sun gives off energy. Machines use energy. Read on to find out more about energy, its forms, how it works, and how it is used.

CHAPTER 1

Fair Fun with Energy

The fair is in town. Farm animals fill the barns. Hungry people drool as they walk past the food stands. Teenagers toss rings and throw darts trying to win prizes. The sounds of talking, laughing, and music buzz all around.

A fair is filled with many types of energy. Being able to see all the food requires light energy. Eating the yummy foods provides energy for the body. Walking and throwing use motion energy. Noises have sound energy.

What is your favorite part of the fair? Is it the food—the hot dogs, ice cream, and cotton candy?

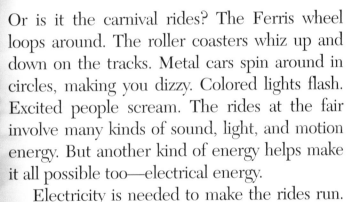

Or is it the carnival rides? The Ferris wheel loops around. The roller coasters whiz up and down on the tracks. Metal cars spin around in circles, making you dizzy. Colored lights flash. Excited people scream. The rides at the fair involve many kinds of sound, light, and motion energy. But another kind of energy helps make it all possible too—electrical energy.

Electricity is needed to make the rides run. Power cords run along the ground, carrying energy to the equipment. Electrical energy powers the bright lights. Motors turn and cause the rides to move. Switches stop the rides so new riders can get on and then start up the fun again for the next group.

The motors that run fair rides have magnets inside them. Without these magnets, the rides would not be able to go up and down or spin around.

The next time you go to the fair, think about what it would be like without electricity and magnets. How much fun would it be without these important sources of energy?

CHAPTER 2

Electricity

They are everywhere! *They* make up the air you breathe, the water you drink, and the food you eat. *They* surround you in your home. *They* are in your floors, furniture, clothing, and pets. *They* even make up you and your family. You cannot escape from *them*. But don't panic. There is no need to worry. What are *they*? *They* are tiny particles called *atoms*, and they make up everything in the world.

Atoms are made up of protons, electrons, and neutrons, which are even smaller particles. Protons have a positive **charge**.

Electrons have a negative charge. Neutrons have no charge. Protons and neutrons are found in the center, or nucleus, of an atom. Electrons travel around the nucleus. Electricity is caused by the movement of these electrons.

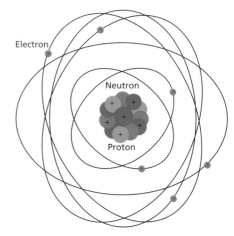

Opposites Attract

Negative charges are attracted, or pulled toward, positive charges. So electrons are attracted to protons. Like charges repel, or push away, from each other. So protons repel protons and electrons repel electrons.

All atoms want to have an equal number of protons and electrons. This will give them a **neutral** charge. Atoms with a neutral charge are called *stable*. All atoms want to be stable. So if an atom has more protons than electrons, it will try to get more electrons. If an atom has more electrons than protons, it will try to give the extra electrons away to other atoms. This transfer or movement of electrons produces electricity.

TWO KINDS OF ELECTRICITY

There are two kinds of electricity—static and current. Static electricity is produced when objects have extra protons or electrons. The object will try to become stable by gaining or losing electrons. When this transfer of electrons happens, electricity is produced.

Try This!

Blow up a balloon and tie it off. Rub the balloon on your hair or clothing. Now hold it up to a wall. What happens?

The balloon will most likely stick to the wall. This is because some electrons from your hair or clothing rubbed off on to the balloon. The balloon now wants to get rid of the extra electrons by giving them to the wall.

Run a comb through your dry hair a few times. Now hold the comb next to a stream of water from a faucet. What happens? Why?

The stream of water will bend toward the comb. This is because the comb picked up extra electrons from your hair. The extra electrons on the comb will pull toward the water in an attempt to give some of the electrons to the water.

Did you ever get a shock when you touched a doorknob? That's because your feet collected electrons from the carpeting. Your body then had a negative charge. These extra electrons jumped to the doorknob when you touched it. This "jumping" movement often results in a little shock. This is static electricity. Sometimes you can even see the spark as the electrons move.

Current electricity is the continuous flow of electrons through a **conductor** such as a wire. This flow of electrons is called a *current*. Current electricity is what runs through cords to power your television, radio, and other electrical appliances.

LIGHTNING

Lightning is static electricity moving between clouds or between clouds and the ground. When water and ice collide inside a cloud, electrical charges are produced. The positive and negative charges separate. When these charges are attracted to opposite charges in other clouds or on the ground, they jump from cloud to cloud, cloud to ground, or ground to cloud. This jumping electricity is the bolt of lightning you see in the sky.

Lightning also strikes other objects to balance its charges. It might strike trees, buildings, water, and sometimes people. Lightning is a very powerful source of electricity.

CHAPTER 3

The Path of Electrons

Electricity can flow through some materials better than others. A material that lets electricity pass through easily is called a *conductor*. Electrons move smoothly through conductors.

Metals are good conductors. Metal wires carry electricity through power lines, homes, businesses, and electrical appliances. Water is also a good conductor, which is why it isn't safe to swim when there's lightning outside.

A material that does not let electricity pass through easily is called an *insulator*. Plastic and rubber are good insulators. Wires are often coated with rubber so the electricity stays inside.

CIRCUITS

The path that electrons follow is called a *circuit*. Electrons leave a power source such as a battery. They travel through a conductor. Most often, metal wires are used. The electricity can power different objects along the circuit. The electrons must complete the circuit by returning to the power source.

If any part of the circuit is broken or not connected, the circuit will not work. Switches can be used to turn circuits on and off. When the switch is on, the electrons move through the circuit. When the switch is off, the circuit is broken, stopping the flow of electricity.

Gas Conductors

Have you ever wondered how store signs with lighted glass tubes work? These signs work because some gases are good conductors. When glass tubes are filled with gas and electricity flows through them, the gases glow. Different gases produce different-colored lights.

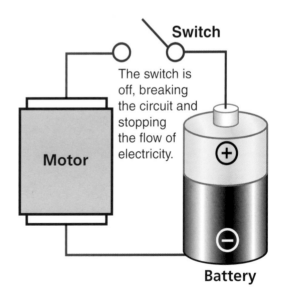

Switch

The switch is off, breaking the circuit and stopping the flow of electricity.

Motor

Battery

Battery Basics

A battery is a power source with chemicals inside. It works by changing chemical energy into electrical energy. Batteries can store their chemical energy for a period of time. When the chemicals have been stored too long or used up, the battery stops working.

Every battery has two electrodes. These are the charged parts of the battery. One electrode has a negative (-) charge. The other electrode has a positive (+) charge.

A battery forms a circuit with the object it's powering. Electrons travel from the battery's negative electrode to wires in the object and back to the battery through the positive electrode.

SERIES CIRCUITS

A series circuit has only one path for electrons to follow. A power source and the object(s) to be powered are connected by a conductor. For example, a battery is hooked to a lightbulb by wires. The electricity flows from the battery through the wires to light the bulb. Then the electricity travels back to the battery.

A series circuit is very simple and easy to make. However, if one part of the circuit breaks down, the flow of electricity stops. The whole circuit will not work.

You may have experienced this with older holiday lights. When one bulb burns out, the whole string of lights goes dark. This is

Series Circuit

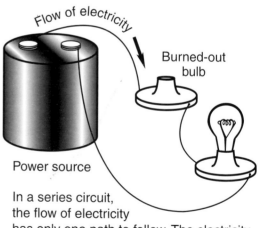

In a series circuit, the flow of electricity has only one path to follow. The electricity cannot flow past the burned-out bulb to light the other bulb.

because the burned-out bulb breaks the circuit. Until you replace the bad bulb, electricity cannot travel to all the other bulbs and back to the power source to complete the circuit.

PARALLEL CIRCUITS

A parallel circuit has more than one path for electrons to follow. One energy source is used, but the wires form more than one path for the electricity to pass through. This means that if one part of the circuit breaks down, the electricity can still get through using a different path. The rest of the circuit will still work.

Newer holiday lights have parallel circuits. So if one bulb burns out, the rest stay lit.

Parallel Circuit

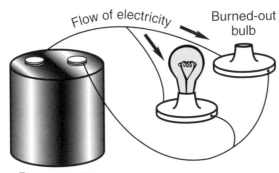

Flow of electricity

Burned-out bulb

Power source

With a parallel circuit, the electrons have more than one path to follow. The flow of electricity can bypass the burned-out bulb to light the other bulb.

Create your own series circuit, and test items to see if they are conductors or insulators.

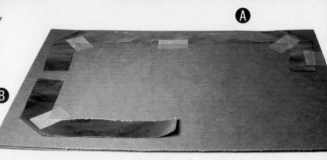

Materials

- 3 strips of aluminum foil about an inch wide (2 strips—8 inches long and 1 strip—16 inches long)
- 2 C or D batteries
- clear tape
- piece of cardboard about the size of a notebook
- flashlight bulb
- clothespin
- rubber band

Procedure

1. Tape the long strip (A) and one of the short strips (B) of foil to the cardboard as shown in the picture.

2. Fold the second short strip (C) in half lengthwise. Wrap one end around the base of the flashlight bulb as shown in the picture.

3. Pinch the base of the bulb in the clothespin. Tape down the clothespin so the base of the bulb touches one end of the long foil strip. (Make sure the foil around the flashlight bulb doesn't touch the strip of foil on the cardboard.)

4. Tape the batteries together so that a positive end is touching a negative end. Tape them to the cardboard between the long strip (A) and short strip (B). Each end of the foil should touch the end of a battery. Wrap the rubber band around the batteries to hold the foil in place.

5. The two loose ends of foil (B and C) are the switch. Touch the ends of the foil together. What happens? The bulb should light up when the switch is closed.

6. To test an item to see if it is a conductor or insulator, place the item between the two open ends and touch each end to the item. If the bulb lights up, then the item is a conductor. If it doesn't light, then the item is an insulator.

CIRCUIT BREAKERS

Have you ever been listening to the radio while drying your hair at the same time your brother is watching TV and your mom is using the electric mixer? Suddenly, the power goes out. Why?

Too much electricity flowing through a circuit can be dangerous. Fires can start when circuits are overloaded. Most homes have circuit breakers to protect against electrical fires.

Circuit breakers open a circuit if too much power is running through it. A fuse is a type of circuit breaker. A fuse has a thin piece of very **resistant** wire running through it. If too much current passes through it, the wire melts. This breaks the circuit. A blown fuse needs to be replaced with a new one before the circuit will work again.

A fuse is a safety device. Within the fuse, a thin piece of foil or wire burns out when too much electric current runs through it. This stops the flow of electricity to prevent the wires from overheating and causing fires.

Each circuit in your house has a circuit breaker or fuse. Newer circuit breakers look like a light switch. They flip off when too much electricity flows through. They can be turned back on over and over again. Houses have many circuits and circuit breakers. The breakers are found in a box on the wall somewhere in the house.

Cars and trucks have fuses too. These fuses protect the circuits powering electrical parts of the car, such as the lights, windshield wipers, radio, and heater.

Ask an adult to show you the fuses in your home and car.

CHAPTER 4
Measuring Electricity

Three different characteristics of electricity can be measured. These are current, voltage, and resistance.

CURRENT

Current is the amount of electricity running through a conductor. It is measured in amps.

Flowing electricity is similar to flowing water. Imagine water flowing through a hose. When using a garden hose, the water current is small. Now imagine a fire hose. It can hold more water, so the water current is greater. Likewise, when using a thin wire, the electrical current is small. A thick electric **cable** can hold a much greater amount of electrical current.

VOLTAGE

Voltage is the force pushing the electricity. It is measured in volts.

To imagine voltage, think about the push behind the water in a hose. The water supply running through a garden hose is small. The force of the water traveling through the hose isn't very large. The force can be controlled somewhat by how much you turn the faucet knob. If you turn it on just a little, the force will be less than when you turn the knob all the way. Either way, the overall force in a garden hose is small.

A garden hose is like a battery. Batteries give electrons a small push. This weak push means low voltage. A normal household battery has low voltage—1.5 to 9 volts.

A fire hydrant has a much larger water supply than a garden hose. This large force gives the water a strong push through a fire hose. A strong push means high voltage. An electrical power plant pushes out high voltages of over 400,000 volts.

Warning—High Voltage!

A "HIGH VOLTAGE" sign on an electrical pole or power station means that a large amount of electricity with great force is flowing in and out of the area. You should stay away from these high voltage areas to avoid shocks, burns, or more serious injuries.

RESISTANCE

Resistance is the force pulling against the flow of electricity. It is measured in ohms.

Resistance can be caused by several things, such as the size or surface of the conductor. A longer hose has more resistance than a shorter hose. There is more hose touching the water and creating **friction** as it moves through. This slows the water down. In a similar way, longer wires create more resistance to the flow of electricity.

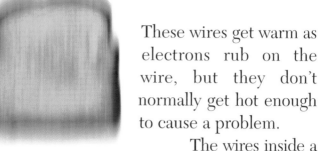

Thinner wires have more resistance than thicker wires. The moving electrons bump into the metal atoms of the wire more frequently in a thin wire since there isn't as much open space for them to travel through. This slows down the electrons and gives off heat as the electrons rub on the walls of the wires.

Thicker wires allow electrons to pass through without hitting the wire's walls as often.

The surface of a conductor also affects resistance. Smooth surfaces allow electrons to pass by quickly and easily. Bumpy or rough surfaces slow electrons down.

Different materials have different amounts of resistance. The copper wires running through your home have little resistance.

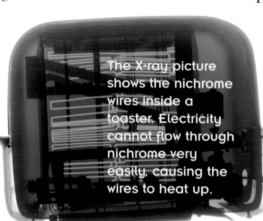

The X-ray picture shows the nichrome wires inside a toaster. Electricity cannot flow through nichrome very easily, causing the wires to heat up.

These wires get warm as electrons rub on the wire, but they don't normally get hot enough to cause a problem.

The wires inside a toaster are made of nichrome (nickel and chromium metals). These thin wires are very resistant to electricity. They heat up so much that they glow a red-orange color. The heat is used to toast your bread.

Highly resistant wires are also used in lightbulbs. A metal called *tungsten* is used in many household lightbulbs. A long, thin strip of tungsten is coiled up to fit inside the bulb. The tungsten is very resistant to electric current. As electricity passes through this wire, it heats up and glows white hot, creating light.

CHAPTER 5
Magnetism

Magnetism is a force that pushes or pulls objects. This force surrounds a magnet in its **magnetic field**. A magnetic field is strongest at the ends, or poles, of the magnet. As you move farther away from a magnet, the field grows weaker.

WHAT IS A MAGNET?

A magnet is an object with a magnetic force. Several metals found in nature are magnetic. Iron, nickel, and cobalt are magnetic metals. Objects made out of these metals are also magnetic.

Particles inside a magnet line up in the same direction at each end. This creates the two strong magnetic poles. In nonmagnetic materials, the particles spread out in all different directions.

Try This!

Not all metals are magnetic. Aluminum is a nonmagnetic metal. A magnet will not pick up aluminum cans.

Test some empty cans from your kitchen. Try to pick up each can using a magnet. Some cans are made of steel, which is a magnetic metal. Others are aluminum. Make a chart that shows which cans are magnetic and which are not.

NORTH AND SOUTH POLES

The poles of a magnet are labeled *north* and *south*. If a magnet is held by a string, the north pole of the magnet will point toward the direction north.

The two poles of a magnet react to each other like positive and negative charges. Opposite poles attract each other. So a north pole and a south pole will pull toward each other. Two like poles will repel, or push away, from each other. So two north poles or two south poles will repel each other. Experiment with different magnets to prove that opposite poles attract and like poles repel.

Try This!

Ask your teacher for some iron filings (shavings). Place a magnet on your desk. Then place a piece of paper or a transparency on top of the magnet. Sprinkle some iron filings on the paper or transparency. Tap the desk lightly. What happens?

The iron filings are attracted to the magnetic field. They should line up in the shape of the magnetic field. More filings will gather in the strongest parts of the field. This should be at the poles of the magnet.

Try different-shaped magnets. Do the magnetic fields change?

PERMANENT OR TEMPORARY?

Some magnets are permanent. This means they keep their magnetism all the time. The magnets you use in science class or at home on your refrigerator are permanent magnets.

Other magnets are temporary. Their magnetic power only lasts for a short time. When a permanent magnet picks up a metal object such as a pin or a nail, the object will act as a magnet. It will be able to pick up other objects. But as soon as the permanent magnet is taken away, the temporary magnet will lose its magnetism.

THE PULL OF THE EARTH

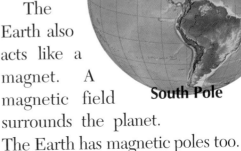

North Pole

South Pole

The Earth also acts like a magnet. A magnetic field surrounds the planet. The Earth has magnetic poles too. These poles are close to the North and South Poles on a map.

Compasses use the magnetic field of the Earth to guide people. One end of a compass needle always points north. By knowing which direction is north, you can figure out the other directions.

Try This!

Gather a few pins or nails. Try to pick up one pin or nail using another. Does it work?

Now use a permanent magnet to pick up a pin or nail. Then try to pick up other pins or nails with the first. Does it work now?

The First Compasses

Early sailors used stars to guide their way at night. But what about during the day or on foggy nights? Then the sailors used lodestones to lead their way. A lodestone is a type of rock with lots of iron in it. This natural magnet acts like a compass needle.

Rub a sewing needle along a permanent magnet in the same direction several times. This will turn the needle into a temporary magnet.

Now push the ends of the needle into two small objects that float, such as corks or marshmallows. Place the floating needle in a pan of water. The needle should be able to float freely in the water without touching the sides of the pan. Watch the needle and record what happens.

The sewing needle is now like a compass needle. Its ends point north and south. Turn the needle the opposite way. The needle should turn itself back. It is being controlled by the Earth's magnetic field.

TYPES OF MAGNETS

Magnets come in a variety of shapes and sizes. The poles on each of these magnets are in different places. Each type of magnet has its own uses.

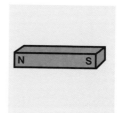

Bar magnets are straight bars shaped liked rectangles. The poles are at opposite ends. Bar magnets are used in compasses and door fasteners.

Horseshoe magnets are in the shape of the letter U. The north and south poles are on each open end. Since the poles are closer together than on a bar magnet, the magnetic field is greater. Horseshoe magnets are used in some small motors.

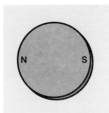

Disk magnets are round and flat. They can have their poles in different places. On some, one pole runs around the edge of the disk while the other pole is in the center. Other disk magnets have their poles on opposite flat sides or on opposite edges. These magnets are used in radio and TV speakers.

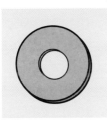

Ring magnets are in a ring or circle shape. These magnets don't have poles. Instead, the magnetism moves around the inside of the ring in one direction. Ring magnets store information in computers.

Rod magnets are shaped like a closed tube, or cylinder. The poles are on each end of the rod. Rod magnets are used to hold magnetic materials in place in some machines.

MAGNETIC LIQUIDS

Did you know that there are even magnetic liquids? They are called *ferrofluids*. Ferrofluids are made of tiny iron particles mixed with water or oil. When a magnet is brought near the liquid, the iron particles become magnetic. The liquid can then move and change shape by following the movement of the magnet.

Ferrofluids were first developed to control the flow of liquid fuels in space. Without gravity, the fuels would float. But a fuel that reacts to a magnet will follow the magnetic field.

Now ferrofluids have many uses. They can work with other magnets to form tight seals on containers to prevent liquids from leaking. They can be used in speakers to produce better sound by absorbing heat and unwanted **vibrations**. Magnetic liquids can also be used to separate waste products, such as **scrap metal**, by pushing different wastes to the surface of the fluid.

CHAPTER 6

How Are They Related?

Electricity and magnetism have a special relationship. Electricity creates a magnetic field. Any material carrying an electric current is surrounded by a magnetic field.

A magnetic field can create electricity. The magnetic field causes the charges inside a wire to separate and move. This flow of charges is electricity.

ELECTROMAGNETS

An electromagnet is a temporary magnet that is turned on and off by electricity. When a current passes through a wire wound into a **coil**, a magnetic field is created. The metal inside the wire coil acts like a magnet. The electromagnet can then attract or repel. When the current is turned off, there is no magnetic field. The electromagnet cannot attract or repel.

A crane is an example of a machine with an electromagnet. When electricity flows through it, the electromagnet on the end of a crane can pick up and move scrap metal. When the electricity is turned off, the metal will drop from the electromagnet.

Electromagnets are found in many household machines. Telephones, doorbells, VCRs, tape players, and computers are just a few machines that use these magnets.

Coiled Wire

A coil of wire that acts like a magnet when electricity runs through it is called a *solenoid*. The coil shape makes the magnetic field stronger than in a straight wire.

With electromagnets, such as those that are used in cranes, it is possible to control the strength of the magnetic field by increasing or decreasing the number of turns or loops in the wire coil.

Try This!

You can make an electromagnet with some simple materials. You will need a large iron nail, some wire, and a battery. Coil the wire around the nail. Attach the ends of the wire to the battery electrodes. Now try to pick up some paper clips or tacks. Remove one end of the wire from the battery and try again. When does the electromagnet work?

A stronger electromagnet should be able to pick up more paper clips or tacks. Try different types of wire or different numbers of coils. Do the wires or number of coils make the electromagnet stronger?

Floating Trains

Maglev trains use electromagnets. Maglev stands for "magnetic **levitation**." This type of train actually floats slightly above the track. The powerful magnets in the train and track repel one another. These trains can move very fast because they don't rub against the track. Adjusting the amount of electricity running through the magnets controls the trains' speed.

MOTORS

A motor is made of magnets and coiled wire. The coiled wire spins. This spinning part of the motor is called a *rotor*. The rotor is located between two or more magnets that don't move. The rotor becomes magnetic when electricity flows through the wire. The electric current going through the wire keeps changing direction. This makes the poles of the rotor keep switching back and forth. The changing poles of the rotor are pushed and pulled by the poles of the other magnets, making the rotor spin. The motor changes electrical energy into motion energy that we can use to do work more easily.

Fans, drills, washers, dryers, food processors, and garbage disposals use the action of rotors to spin. Vacuum cleaners, refrigerators, TVs, and cars have motors. Moving machines such as conveyor belts, escalators, and elevators also have motors. Your life would move in slow (or no) motion without motors.

John Logie Baird (1888–1946) gave the first public showing of mechanical television on January 26, 1926, at Selfridge's Department Store in London. By September 1929, the BBC (British Broadcasting Company) began regular experimental TV broadcasts using Baird's invention. Wouldn't Baird be surprised at how popular his invention is and how much it has changed!

GENERATORS AND POWER PLANTS

A generator creates electricity. Power plants use generators to make large quantities of electricity.

How does a generator work? A spinning magnet inside coils of wire changes motion energy into electrical energy. Sometimes the coils of wire spin inside the magnets. Either way, when the coils turn in the magnetic field, electricity is produced.

How is the spinning motion produced? Most power plants turn chemical energy into electrical energy. They burn **fossil fuels** to release energy. The heat produced when fossil fuels are burned is used to change water into steam. The steam is used to turn large fan blades called *turbines*. Rods attached to the turbines turn inside a generator. These metal rods are usually made up of many wire coils. Large magnets surround the coils. As the coils turn inside the magnetic field, electricity is created. It then travels out the wire coils to power lines.

Hydroelectric turbine generators

Wind turbines use wind energy to create electricity. Wind is a renewable energy source.

Not all power plants burn fossil fuels for energy. Some plants use wind, water, or **solar** energy to turn the turbines. Nuclear power plants use materials that break down and release large amounts of heat. The heat is used to make steam to move the turbines.

Power plants make electricity for communities. The electricity is then sent out through power lines to be used in homes, schools, and businesses.

More or Less Power

Transformers are machines that change the amount of voltage traveling through the lines. Some transformers increase the voltage. They are used to send the electricity across longer distances. Other transformers decrease the voltage. They are used to lessen the power before it goes into your home.

Some power lines are aboveground. Other power lines run under the ground. The power lines make a complete circuit. The circuit starts at the power plant. Then the power lines go out to many different power stations. These stations run power lines to homes, schools, and businesses in an area. The power lines also carry electricity back to the power stations and power plant, completing the circuit.

The electricity that leaves the power plant and moves to the power substation is high voltage so that it can travel long distances. Transformers change the electricity from high to low voltage before power lines carry the electricity to your home.

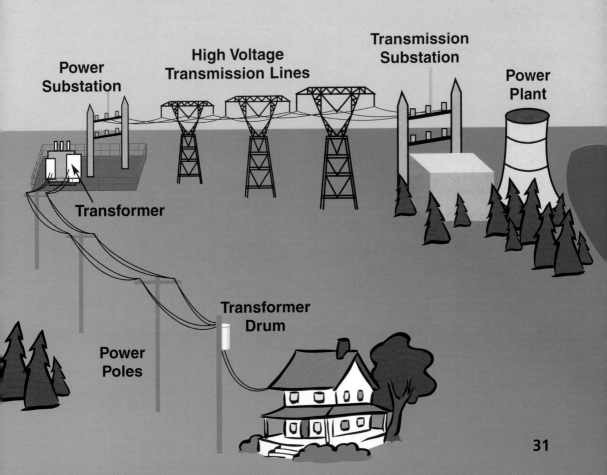

Power Substation

High Voltage Transmission Lines

Transmission Substation

Power Plant

Transformer

Transformer Drum

Power Poles

CHAPTER 7

Electricity and Magnetism Scientists

BEN FRANKLIN

One scientist who usually comes to mind when people think about electricity is Ben Franklin. In 1752, Franklin flew a kite during an electrical storm. A key was attached to the kite string. When the kite was struck by lightning, the lightning traveled down the string to the metal key. This produced a spark. Franklin's kite experiment proved that lightning is electricity.

Franklin also invented the lightning rod. A lightning rod gives lightning a safe path from the top of a building down to the ground. It protects buildings from burning when struck by lightning.

Lightning strikes the lightning rod, not the house, protecting the building from damage. Ben Franklin thought a pointed lightning rod was the better design, but it has now been proven that rods with blunt, rounded ends provide more protection.

Ben Franklin

ALESSANDRO VOLTA

Alessandro Volta invented the first battery in 1800. Volta's battery was important because it helped other scientists do more experiments with electricity. Scientists could now produce electricity easily. The volt used to measure voltage is named for this battery inventor.

Alessandro Volta

HANS CHRISTIAN OERSTED

In 1820, Hans Christian Oersted made a very important discovery by accident. At the time, Oersted was teaching a college science class. While doing an experiment, Oersted noticed that the needle of a compass moved every time a wire with electrical current flowing through it was near. His discovery proved that an electric current creates a magnetic field. The electromagnet and motor were invented soon after.

Hans Christian Oersted

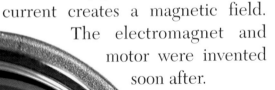

In a magnetic compass, a magnet, which is the needle of the compass, is balanced on a pivot at the center so that the needle can swing freely. The magnetic field of the Earth causes the needle to always point north.

33

MICHAEL FARADAY

In 1831, Michael Faraday recognized that a magnetic field could create electricity. Faraday was repeating Oersted's experiment with electricity and magnetism. When he added another wire to the magnetic field, a current started flowing through it too. Since that wire wasn't hooked up to a power source, Faraday realized that magnetism must have caused the electric current. The invention of the generator and motor were based on Faraday's discovery.

THOMAS EDISON

Another scientist that people usually think of when they think of electricity is Thomas Edison. Edison invented the lightbulb in 1878. He also worked to perfect the electric generator. In 1882, he established the first power station and electricity system in New York City.

CHAPTER 8

Everyday Electricity and Magnetism

Did you know that about four out of every ten people in the world do not have electricity where they live? Imagine a day in your life without electricity—no lights, no TV, no radios, no video games. Is it shocking?

And what about magnetism? It's not just something fun to experiment with in school or use to hold up your photos and art projects on the refrigerator. Have you ever thought about the magnet inside the refrigerator that holds the door shut or the thousands of magnets inside machines that make your daily life easier?

Animal Magnetism

Magnetism isn't just important to people. It helps other creatures too. Animals that travel over long distances use magnetism. Monarch butterflies, whales, sea turtles, and many birds **migrate**. It is believed that tiny particles of iron in their brains act like compasses to guide them in the right direction.

Think about entertainment in your world. The music you enjoy comes from a radio or CD player that runs thanks to electricity and magnetism. The videos you watch have magnetic patterns on them. These patterns hold the information that you see and hear. The VCR "reads" these patterns and turns them into the movies you watch.

The invention of electricity and its relationship to magnetism light up your world. Almost everything you do depends on these amazing energy sources. So be thankful for those little particles called electrons and the power they provide!

Try This!

Keep track of all the ways you use electricity and magnetism in a day. Compare your list with other classmates' lists. Combine lists to make one class list of the electricity and magnetism found in your everyday life. Can you imagine a world without these two sources of energy?

INTERNET CONNECTIONS AND RELATED READING FOR ELECTRICITY AND MAGNETISM

Energy Quest (http://www.energyquest.ca.gov/index.html)
This fun site provides information, stories, news, projects, games, and links to other energy sites. Visit the Gallery of Energy Pioneers too.

How Stuff Works (http://www.howstuffworks.com or http://www.howstuffworks.com/electromagnet.htm)
If you have questions about how anything involving energy, electricity, magnets, and electromagnets work, these Web sites are the places to look.

Energy Information Administration (http://www.eia.doe.gov/kids/index.html)
Review the definition of energy and its forms here. Then check out the Kid's Corner, Fun Facts, and Energy Quiz.

U.S. Department of Energy (http://www.eere.energy.gov/kids/)
Dr. E's Energy Lab will teach you about solar energy and energy efficiency. A dog named Roofus shows you his energy-efficient home and neighborhood. Many links to other energy sites can be found here.

The Atoms Family (http://www.miamisci.org/af/sln)
This spooky Web site teaches about different forms of energy through simple experiments.

One World.Net's Kid's Channel (http://www.oneworld.net/penguin/energy/energy.html)
Tiki the Penguin discusses the positive and negative sides of different types of energy sources.

Discovering Electricity by Rae Bains. Young readers discover what makes electricity and how it is carried, used, and measured. Troll, 1982. [RL 3 IL 2–4] (4129101 PB)

Electricity by Steve Parker. An Eyewitness Science book on electricity. Dorling Kindersley, 1992. [RL 8.5 IL 3–8] (5868406 HB)

Electricity by Darlene Lauw and Lim Cheng Puay. Presents activities that demonstrate how electricity works in our everyday lives. History boxes feature the scientists who made significant discoveries in the field of electricity. Crabtree Publishing, 2002. [RL 4.2 IL 2–5] (3396801 PB)

Energy by Jack Challoner. An Eyewitness Science book on energy. Dorling Kindersley, 1993. [RL 7.9 IL 3–8] (5868606 HB)

Energy by Alvin and Virginia Silverstein and Laura Silverstein Nunn. Explains a fundamental concept of science, gives some background, and discusses current applications and developments. Millbrook Press, 1998. [RL 5 IL 5–8] (3111906 HB)

Lightning by Seymour Simon. An introduction to lightning, one of nature's most fierce and mysterious forces. William Morrow, 1997. [RL 4 IL 2–5] (3277101 PB 3277102 CC)

The Magic School Bus and the Electric Field Trip by Joanna Cole. A thunderstorm and a blackout send Ms. Frizzle and her class on an electrifying field trip to see how electricity functions. Scholastic, 1997. [RL 3.4 IL 1–4] (5950501 PB 5950502 CC)

Magnets by Darlene Lauw and Lim Cheng Puay. Introduces the concept of magnetism through various activities and projects. Crabtree Publishing, 2002. [RL 3.5 IL 2–5] (3396301 PB)

- RL = Reading Level
- IL = Interest Level

Perfection Learning's catalog numbers are included for your ordering convenience. PB indicates paperback. HB indicates hardback.

GLOSSARY

cable (KAY buhl) group of wires

charge (charj) amount of electricity

coil (koyl) loop or spiral

conductor (kuhn DUHK ter) material that lets electricity flow through easily

fossil fuel (FAH suhl fyoul) fuel, such as coal, oil, and natural gas, formed in the earth from the remains of dead plants and animals

friction (FRIK shuhn) force between two rubbing objects that acts against motion

levitation (lev uh TAY shuhn) act of rising or floating in the air

magnetic field (mag NET ik feeld) area around a magnet where the force of magnetism exists

migrate (MEYE grayt) to move from one region or climate to another, usually in search of warmer weather and food

neutral (NOO truhl) neither positive nor negative

resistant (ree ZIS tent) not allowing electricity to pass through easily

scrap metal (skrap MET uhl) metal pieces or parts that have been thrown out and are only useful in recycling

solar (SOH ler) coming from the sun

theory (THEAR ee) belief that has been scientifically tested to the point of being accepted as true by most people

vibration (veye BRAY shuhn) back and forth movement

INDEX

_____